God's Baby Girl

Tiane Sutton

www.hisglorycreationspublishing.com

Copyright © 2020 by Tiane Sutton

All rights reserved. No part of this book may be reproduced in any form without permission in writing from the publisher, except in the case of brief quotations embodied in critical articles or reviews. Unauthorized reproduction of any part of this work is illegal and is punishable by law. The author and publisher shall have neither liability nor responsibility for anyone with respect to any loss or damage caused directly or indirectly, by the information contained in this book.

ISBN: 978-1-950861-16-3

Scripture references are used with permission from Zondervan via Biblegateway.com

Cover Photos: David Scott, Heatvizion Photography

Printed in the United States of America

Dedication

THIS BOOK IS DEDICATED TO JUSTIN T. COLEMAN

Contents

Preface 7

Acknowledgements.. 9

Foreword 11

Introduction 13

Part One: Kindred Spirits

Chapter 1: Angela 17

Chapter 2: Brenda 21

Chapter 3: Jenna 25

Chapter 4: Ishma 29

Chapter 5: Ada 33

Chapter 6: Hannah 39

Chapter 7: Margaret 43

Part Two: God's Baby Girl

Chapter 8: God's Baby Girl 49

Chapter 9: Forgiveness 53

Chapter 10: Abstinence 57

Chapter 11: Salvation 63

Chapter 12: Who is God's Baby Girl? 67

Notes 71

About the Author 101

Preface

CONVICTIONS ARE SUCH BEAUTIFUL THINGS with so much potential to manifest into blessings. Truly amazing. Merriam-Webster defines this transforming word as the state of being convinced of error or compelled to admit the truth. This book was created because of that: the state of being convinced of error or compelled to admit the truth. See this was my first known interaction with God in my new found faith. May 17th, 2018 was a day to remember. I will go into further details about how it all led to this day later in the book. That was the day I accepted Jesus Christ as my Lord and Savior. I was sitting in a random woman's car praying for the first time in my life to a God I was taught to never believe in. I was raised atheist, and no, I didn't worship Satan. He was not real to me, just like God wasn't. I was a regular person living a pretty average life and thought I was living by the book, actually. Once saved, I quickly realized that I was making a mistake.

Convictions. It is how I became who I am today. My relationship with God was horrible at this point of newly being saved. There was only one real way I found how to show obedience, love, respect, and trust for God. I had to save my body, sexually, for marriage. At that point, that was how I was living in sin. My ex and I were sort of living together, and we knew each other for 8 years prior to this convicting moment, so that transition was not easy, to say the least. I was so ashamed of how I used God's name in vain and took every chance I had to try to teach people why they should not believe in such a "fictional character." All I wanted was to thank God for waiting for me and welcoming me into an eternity of joy. Once convicted to become abstinent, I had a series of events that happened to me immediately that made me feel punished for choosing God. I felt so helpless, lonely, and worthless for a while. I did not know how to turn my life around. I only knew how to be faithful and loyal to him by not having sex, so I focused on the one thing I can control, my actions. My relationship with God increased, and I fell in love with Jesus so much. I firmly believe that he saw that he could trust me with abstinence, so he blessed me with another conviction. Blessed? I took a second to ponder on that adjective because this was when I realized my purpose.

The word "conviction" almost has this bitter and cringe-worthy taste to it. It's like we already know we will have to feel pain, sacrifice something, and go through a mundane journey. However, it really is such a beautiful thing with so much potential to be a pivotal event in life, when God is involved, and we are obedient to the conviction. My decision to wait until marriage for sex had tremendous results—so many blessings and miracles that I cannot even begin to list. I learned to love that heavy weight on my shoulders, also known as conviction. God convicted me during these times to share the gospel, specifically through my life's testimony. This book was started in 2018 and brought to completion in 2020. I am using this book as a platform to be obedient to that conviction. God's Baby Girl will open your heart to the world around us. I walk through my life experiences through the eyes of other women. This represents how all people go through hardships in life, even if they still think they are the only ones with problems. God loves all his sons and daughters and has a specific plan to allow us to live in our fullest potential while here in this lifetime. I believe as you read this book, you will look at your struggling times differently, and you will gain mental stability to help you move past childhood hardships. I truly pray that you look at any "conviction" you believe God placed on your heart as an opportunity to prove your trust and love for God by being obedient to that. Enjoy this book! After all, it's about you.

Acknowledgements

I would like to thank a couple of people for making this book a reality for me. First, my husband Marquise. My desire to write this book came before I met Mr. Sutton. However, he helped me believe in myself and take that first leap to actually commit. I know that I would not have completed this book as soon as I did if he was not there encouraging me and helping me set my priorities, completing this project.

Second, I would like to thank my publisher Minister Felicia Lucas. Sure, she is doing her "job," and I am paying for this exact service. However, I specifically chose Mrs. Lucas because of her relationship with God through Christ. Her publishing company is called His Glory Creations Publishing, which was the first spiritual confirmation I had to even write this book.

Third, I'd like to thank everyone that has been involved with any photoshoots, writing, brainstorming and promotion of God's Baby Girl. It is a challenge to name everyone without the fear of missing anyone, so just know if you had a part in the making of this book, I greatly appreciate you.

Fourth, I would like to thank my parents, Esmeralda and Thomas. As you read this book, you will see that I did not have the best childhood growing up. However, I thank both of my parents dearly for raising me to be the wise young lady I am. We've had trials and tribulations, but that was before King Jesus, amen. Now we are joined together most of the time, glorifying the Lord and serving his kingdom.

Fifth, I would like to thank my older brother, Justin Coleman. Yes, I also dedicated this book to him. Justin has always made me feel safe to take my own path. No, he did not always support "my own" path sometimes, especially when it involved boys, but he did ensure that he would not let anything harmful happen to me. He is a protector and defender and has a beautiful spirit that's passion filled. That's where I think I get my boldness from!

Lastly, I would like to thank Lisa Bauer. She has not only led me to Christ but helped me ease my way into a newfound life. I started to go to counseling and met an amazing woman named Robin Rosario! Lisa showed me how to live for God. She is the one that educated me on sexual immortalities. That woman is a true servant of the Lord! These people helped me to this point, and I now thank you. Reader, you are a part of my journey as well, and I pray you receive something of value from this journey!

Foreword

By Lisa Bauer

WHAT A TIMELY MESSAGE! In a world of uncertainty about what is true, this is a must-read for any woman who wants a life of truth and purpose. The journey from where we are to who we are meant to be can be found in the quest for truth. And when you find it, all of life becomes clear, and you then have a foundation to stand on as you live the life you were meant to live. One spring day, I sat across a lunch table with Tiane and listened as she asked many questions about religion, faith, the bible and Jesus. Tiane shared about currently hearing people at work who would speak of their faith in Jesus and how their life was different. This caused her to begin to think about her own life, what is it supposed to look like? Tiane grew up in a home where she was confused about what real love looked like. Trusting someone was difficult, and Tiane had reached the place in her life where she was seeking her own identity, asking the questions, who am I? What do I believe? Who do I want to become? In her search for truth, Tiane peeled back the layers of an atheistic viewpoint taught to her and a religion filled with rules and rituals and found that the words in the bible rang true. That day, Tiane met Jesus Christ, who came to her in a personal way, and she has never looked back. Her story unveils the journey of a young girl who encounters "a man" and becomes a woman who finds truth, identity and purpose just by saying, yes!

Introduction

Let me take you on a journey…a journey that explains how I transformed my spirituality from atheism to Christianity. I was raised in the South Bronx, New York, surrounded by a hectic culture. People of color were often mistreated by police, housing conditions were belittling, and crime rates seemed to always be on the rise. Some people, in the middle of this systematic generational oppression, were able to find a sense of hope, understanding of the world, and enlightenment through a movement called 5 Percent Nation. For my immediate family, we found that sense of hope too, as 5 percenters. The leaders taught so many empowering things from self-worth to community unity. However, it was a practice that denounced all religions with Christianity as the most discredited.

At the age of 22, I turned my back on that movement to build a relationship with my Lord and Savior Jesus Christ. My testimony includes life events that helped this transition. In this book, I will be walking you through pivotal moments that took place in my life. However, it will be written in the eyes of other ladies: Angela, she will represent the bullying in school I went through. Brenda, the sexual abuse that scarred me for a while. Jenna, for the time I was homeless. Ishma, she will represent how I was as an atheist and my thought process then. Ada, representing dating relationships. Hannah, for all the ways Mom pushed me to try new things, and Margaret, she will represent when I gave my life to Christ.

My point for that is for many reasons. First, to bring awareness to the constant occurrence of abuse that many people go through in their childhood or adult lives but feel alone and don't speak about it. The second reason is to explain and broadcast God's love for all people, even those who don't know him. Lastly, I am still on my journey with learning who God is and how he sees me, so I am being obedient to him by completing this book. Please enjoy as I introduce the series of events that I went through in my life with my kindred spirits in part one, and part two will be a conference wrapping all my thoughts of the life events into a meaningful discussion.

Part One:
Kindred Spirits

Chapter 1

ANGELA

Count it all joy, my brothers, when you meet trials of various kinds. - James 1:2

On a cool fall morning, Angela, mainly known as Angie, was excited for another day at school. She looked forward to seeing all her friends. Dressed in her white polo shirt and navy-blue skirt, finished with long white tube socks and shiny black shoes, she was ready to conquer the day. She was greeted in the cafeteria by one of her friend's name Bianca. Bianca was not in the best mood. She didn't like how happy and confident Angie was. Bianca snaps, "what are you smiling at?" Angie knew it was wise to lose the smirk and reply nothing. Angela gave an eye roll to the nearest smiling face just to be on Bianca's side. Bianca left Angie and sat at their normal table to eat breakfast. Angie forces her angry face for a while just in case Bianca was still looking at her, and while doing so, she whispered to herself, "it's going to be a good day," that was reassuring. Walking to the table where Bianca was sitting, she was confronted by a girl, and it was another one of her friends. She said, "I don't like the way you walk. You look, bougie." This was Tiffany, and that's how she welcomed Angie to sit at the table.

Before Angie could respond, she immediately realizes that she was different. Angela compared herself and was confused. Skin color is the same, check. She listened for a second, and she talked like them too, with a sharp New York accent. You know, the type where the words "part" and "pot" sound the exact same, check. As Angela was struggling to figure out what made her different, Brittany helped her because she was another friend at the table. Brittany aggressively stroked her fingers through Angela's curly and tangled hair. The thought came as Angela let out a huge "ouch!" As her friends laughed, she noticed she couldn't do it back to them because their hair was straight. Not naturally straight, they had kinky hair, but when it was treated with harsh chemicals to strip the MotherLand roots away, it became straight. "It's going to be a good day," she mumbled under her breath as she finished her breakfast and headed to class. "Finally," Angie was exhausted.

School was over, and now she could hang out with her neighborhood friends! Angie lived in a pretty dangerous and unpredictable neighborhood. Luckily, her family members have something called "street credibility," and they made it safe for her. She walked past a family friend and would typically say hi, but this time he looked a bit different. His face was leatherier and more irritated than normal. His eyes were pretty dilated, and he also was swaying a lot. Angela knew it was best she didn't engage, so she kept walking by.

She passed a local bodega where she got a warm welcome from the clerk "hola amiga," he shouted as he pushed the overweight cat off the loaves of bread. Angela grabbed her usual quarter water, bread and butter and headed home. She passed a memorial of a little girl's face painted on the entire wall of the building. The young girl was murdered because of family affairs, and the community wanted to give respect with the painting. Angela counted her blessings and ran across the street to her building. After walking up four flights of steps, she's home! Angela threw her bag down, ate her snack, and ran across the hallway to her friend's Margarita's house. To her surprise, another one of her friends, Marcella, was there too! "How awesome?!" The girls were enjoying some music videos, and Angela was having a bit of a struggle keeping up. The songs were all in Spanish, and although she was half

Puerto Rican, she didn't speak fluently in Spanish, so her mind was overwhelmed with the translating she had to do.

Angela was trying her best to sing along. After all, she was outnumbered and, once again, the outcast. The girls cut their eyes at her and noticed Angela's insecurities. They chuckled and shared a few comments with each other. Of course, that made Angela even more uncomfortable. Angela almost lost her positivity, but she thought to herself, "it's going to be a good day." Margarita and Marcella continued to converse in Spanish even though their friend couldn't keep up. Angela began to feel awkward, and she didn't understand why there was nobody like her. At school, she felt like she stood out because her appearance was different from her friends and her positive personality. Back home, she was left out sometimes because she wasn't as exposed to her culture as most of her friends were. She looked around the room as if she was going to get a clue, and to her surprise, she did.

She noticed her parents were the only real interracial couple around, and that made her mixed. Wouldn't this mean she gets the best of both worlds? Wrong. At least that's what Angela thought. She just didn't feel welcomed and was bullied everywhere she went. After going back home, Angela sat in her room alone. She looked across the room at her childhood book: The Ugly Duckling. She suddenly pouted and lost all sense of value. "What use am I if I don't fit in anywhere?" Angela's mom walked in right on time and presented her with a penny.

With her mom's intuition, she said, "you see this penny?" Angela looked and nodded, yes. "It doesn't look green or like paper, like dollars or silver like the rest of the coins, but it is still money." Angela was waiting for her mom's wisdom to make sense of this analogy to life. "Although it's not like the others, doesn't mean it doesn't add value. In fact, this penny is the most valuable. It stands out. You can replace all other coins and bills with a penny, but you cannot replace a penny with any other coin or bill." "Angela sweetheart, what makes you not fit in is the same thing that makes you stand out. Your beautiful caramel skin and long curly hair gives you this unique beauty that makes the world stop and stare. Your ethnicity is something most people wished they could understand and experience. Being mixed is a gift of perspective. You see the lifestyles of two different cultures.

Anyone can learn a language, even you." Angela laughed, "Mom, you must've read the ugly duckling recently, huh?" "No honey, I read a better book that said 'what the devil can't destroy, he'll distract. And he can't destroy you, so he tries and distracts you from your true beauty, and you can't operate in your full potential if you're feeling less of the person God created you to be." Angela began to actually hear her mom, "you have to understand that you will never please everyone, and there is only one perfect person who's not you," she said with a chuckle as she brushes Angela's hair. "You need to keep that positive attitude I know you have and never forget that God does not make mistakes. And--" Angela interrupts her mom, "Okaaaaay Mom, thank you. I am happy again. Sheesh! Don't start preaching," they both started laughing, and her mom said, "Okay baby, just don't let any energy that's not of God fill your heart and distract your mind." Angela knew she needed to change the topic, pronto. "Mom, did you check the mail?" Angela has been waiting for an acceptance letter to this retreat next summer! Her mom slowly replied to create a dramatic effect. "Yes...I... did, are you looking for this?" She waived the letter above Angie's head and screamed, "YOU GOT IN!" Angela was so grateful that the girls' group at school held that raffle for the ticket, and her submission won! "God's Baby Girl, summer 21' here I come!" Angela whispered to herself with a smile, "it was a good day."

Chapter 2

BRENDA

Finally, be strong in the Lord and in the strength of his might. Put on the whole armor of God that you may be able to stand against the schemes of the devil.
- Ephesians 6:10-11

Here was a girl, shaking uncontrollably in her bathroom. She's reflecting on the day and began wondering how she was going to tell her mom what happened. It was the first day of middle school. She was so excited! Dressed for a successful new beginning, Brenda was headed to school. While at school, Brenda began to experience some stomach pain. She never felt this uncomfortable and sick before. She rested her head on the desk, but that didn't last long. She was suddenly interrupted. "Brenda, get your head off the desk please," her teacher shouted from across the room. "I'm sorry Mrs. Williams. I just don't feel good," Brenda replied, hoping she will get a pass to put her head down again. Brenda clenched her fist to endure the pain. Finally, she had enough of the pain and decided to leave school and walk home.

On her very long walk home, the pain grew and grew. "What did I eat?" Brenda asked herself as she took a mental inventory of what could be in her stomach. Brenda finally made it home and rushed to the bathroom. Frantic, she shouted, "I'm bleeding!!!" Brenda immediately called her mom. She had a huge emergency and didn't want to bleed out and die. While panicking, she overhears her mom laughing on the phone. "Oh baby, you'll be fine. You just started your menstrual cycle… your period girl. Take some Ibuprofen in the medicine cabinet and get a nap. When you wake up, the pain will be gone." "Wow," Brenda thought, "this is what it feels like to be a woman." She laughed at herself for panicking like she was actually going to die!

Brenda did as her mom told her and felt at ease replaying her mom's words, "when you wake up, the pain will be gone." Her mom did not know the indescribable pain that will come once she awakes. Brenda fell asleep in the living room on the couch. "Wait, what's going on? Am I dreaming? Is this sleep paralysis?" Brenda asked herself as she was lying there, unable to move. It became clear that she was awake, and this was real. A nightmare would have been much more bearable. Sadly, this monster was real. "Did I leave the door unlocked? I hope he doesn't hurt me." Brenda was stuck, trying to understand what she was going through. She was growing more and more shocked as she became familiar with the scent of the man that was sexually molesting her. His body was overwhelmingly holding her down, unable to maneuver. His hands were freezing cold as they were underneath her clothes, groping and grabbing places no-one has ever touched but her. Her heart began to beat fast, and she realized the monster taking advantage of her was her father. The man who raised her and was her best friend until now. "Is this really happening? Is this what happens when you become a woman? Wait, does he know what is going on down there? Am I supposed to move, or do I let him finish? Does he know I am awake?"

Brenda was stuck, and her mind was racing. While he was stripping her literally and figuratively of her innocence, Brenda was just lying there feeling worthless and helpless. She was stuck for what felt like an eternity. She mustered up enough courage to adjust herself in a natural way to make it seem like she was still sleeping. That gave Brenda's dad a hint, and he quickly got off the couch. She began to think again, "how many times has this happened? Should I tell Mom? Is this normal? Was he mad at me? That must be it. There's no way he would do that to me if he was not mad at me."

Brenda was still pretending to be asleep, but she was wide awake at this point. Her mind was racing, and it was time to act now. He was gone. She had to start rationalizing what could happen if she told someone, and he got in trouble. "If I tell anyone about this, then my family would be mad at me for embarrassing them. If my dad goes to jail for this, then my brothers are not going to have their dad in their lives. My dad might even have a hard time in jail, and he will be so lonely in that place.

Brenda, without even knowing, had her priorities set around everything other than herself. She couldn't think about the unfair, illegal, and damaging treatment she got but did not deserve. She placed her family's image, her brother's relationship with that man, and her victimizer's comfortability above her own self-respect, self-love, and protection. There are many variables as to why this was her thought process. A possible variable is because she's black. Black girls are not represented in her country as valuable and precious as a white girl. So why would she see herself as someone that is worth the justice? Another possible variable is that she came to a very clear conclusion that if she was not important enough to be molested in the first place, then she was definitely not important enough to seek healing from this trauma.

See, Brenda judged the actions of someone else as the direct depiction of her worth. How her father treated her was what conditioned her perspective of her self-worth. A last possible variable is that she was scared. What if this was normal? What if her mom got angry at her? What if her dad got mad and did worse to her? Brenda didn't understand the situation she was in and scared herself immediately out of thinking about why she should speak out. So, she decided to act like it never happened.

This really hurt Brenda because now she was no longer excited and didn't know how to tell her parents about her acceptance letter. She was finally accepted to a cool girls' retreat coming up next summer. She closed her eyes and began to listen to a voice in her head saying, "Have faith, my child, you will come out of this darkness, you will prosper and this is a test to go with your testimony." She left the letter on the kitchen counter and locked herself in her room. Shocked and unable to contain herself, she went to her bathroom to cry. She heard her mom come home... Here was a girl, shaking uncontrollably in her bathroom. She was reflecting on the day and wondered how she was going to tell her mom what happened. Brenda wiped her tears and left the bathroom. She greeted her mom with a big smile, "Mom! I got accepted!" It won't be that bad to hold it in and act like it never happened. Would it?

Chapter 3

Jenna

Trust in the LORD with all your heart and lean not on your own understanding. - Proverbs 3:5-6

Jenna was staring out the window extremely excited about this new adventure. Mom and Dad were in front navigating, and her two smelly brothers were making a very uncomfortable smelly sandwich on either side of her. They were heading down south, whatever that meant; all she knew was New York City. She thought about all the cool country friends with their funny accents and big smiles she might have now. As they were traveling, the family stopped at a rest area to freshen up and stretch. Jenna overheard her parents, arguing as she was leaving the bathroom. She couldn't piece together what it was about, but she knew they were worried about something. Jenna ignored that thought and decided to entertain herself by getting on social media to show off her new life.

They finally got to their destination and went to a neighborhood restaurant. "Mom, what's wrong?" Jenna interrupted the facade of peace her mom had. Dad and the boys went to the bathroom, and Jenna saw the perfect opportunity to bring up that argument from earlier. "Things are going to be different, baby," her mom continued to explain after taking a deep breath, "we will still be happy, but we will not have our own place to call home right away." Jenna was confused, so her mom went deeper into explanation. "I mean, there is no home here. There's a community of good people that'll help us get on our feet. We will be living with them until we could afford our own. I do not want you to worry, though. That's why your father and I didn't tell you guys anything."

Mom pointed at Jenna with her fork, letting her know to drop the conversation. Her dad and brothers got back to the table from the bathroom and she had no choice but to play along and "not worry." Jenna was shocked the rest of the night though. The family rushed downtown. Her parents were extra anxious. They parked and quickly jumped out of the car. Jenna and family rushed towards this big brown building, and there was a line that was running low at the door. As soon as they got inside, she saw that the line they were standing in was the "sleep for a night" line, and if you were not in the doors by 7 pm, then you were not allowed into the homeless shelter. Jenna experienced so much chaos in one moment. Her dad and oldest brother were separated immediately. She saw them go downstairs and had no idea what happened to them. Jenna was scared at this point; it was only Mom and Baby brother.

They were taken into this very large room. It almost looked like a gymnasium. She noticed that in this room, there were skinny blue cots to use as beds, and the room was filled with other women and kids. "Mom, are we supposed to sleep here with all these strangers?" Her mom ignored her to avoid the embarrassment. Instead, she went to thank the lady that guided them to the room. They began to unpack their belongings, making sure it doesn't pass their cots line invading someone else's space. "Mom, this is scary," Jenna noticed some of the women were crying, talking to themselves, and just silently staring at her. "This is temporary Jenna; I need you to be strong. Just lay here and look at me for the rest of the night, nothing else, to forget that you are here."

Jenna laid towards her mom and looked at her tired eyes until she fell asleep. "Mom didn't want this for us..." she thought. Soon she was finally asleep. At 4 am, all the lights in the gym cut on. "Good morning, ladies. Please quickly gather your belongings and start a line in the restroom. I need you all out of the building with no excuses by 7 am!"

Jenna was scared out of her sleep and began to panic again. What she thought was a nightmare was confirmed to be reality. Jenna grabbed the basket that was given to her with toiletries in them. Then she stood in line to use the shower. It looked like a locker room or what the inside of a jail bathroom might look like. Everything was out in the open for all the strangers to see. Sinks were linked together side by side down the wall. The stalls had somewhat of a door and the showers were much better without the dirty shower curtains.

Once they finished that routine, they were guided to the basement level. Jenna noticed what looked like a kitchen and a dining room. "Mom!" Jenna's older brother yelled from across the room. The family was finally reunited, and it seemed like nobody wanted to share their experience from last night. They ate quickly, and like the lady said at 4 am, they were out of there with no excuse before 7 am. Once she was outside, Jenna looked around and mumbled " So what now, Mom? Where do we go from here, and you do not want me to worry?" This was the start to a long painful journey of being homeless for 2 years.

A couple of months of every night being separated with her dad and big brother, Jenna's mom put her and her older brother in a group home so they could be together and have each other's back. The sacrifice of doing that meant that Jenna's mom and baby brother were stuck in that shelter alone. One day, Jenna was especially hurt because she had a curfew at the group home at 6 pm. Her mom was spending some quality time with her and then it felt as if someone stole the time right out of their day. Jenna's mom took a bus back to the shelter from Jenna's group home and the stop was right across the street from the house. Once they said their goodbyes, Jenna and her older brother watched as their mom and little brother crossed the street and waited for the bus. She watched her mom cry behind her little brother's back, like she was ashamed of what she was putting her children through. Jenna ran upstairs to the shared bedroom and wept to sleep.

Jenna woke up to a counselor from the group home. "Hey sweetie, my name is Rebecca Hotwaters". Jenna, uncertain as to why she woke her up, was polite and responded, "Hi Rebecca". " I just came in the check on you, I saw you watch your mom leave. I am so sorry you're going through this. You are such a good kid and it may feel like you're out of place." Jenna looked out the window and said quietly, "yeah, I am not like these girls here, I didn't get in trouble and I'm still being punished." Rebecca reached in her back pocket and as she was pulling out a brochure, she said "I believe you Jenna. However, you have to embrace this season of life you're in.

This is a brochure to a ladies conference coming up summer 2021. It's called God's Baby Girl and there you can find your purpose and share your testimony for other little girls in places they don't feel they belong. If you get yourself through these hard times and make it to this conference, I believe doors will open for you like you can't imagine." Jenna smiled at the thought of having a brighter future but then she frowned. "Rebecca... my mom doesn't have the money for this, so I don't see that happening for me." Rebecca grabbed Jenna's hand and said "I'll pay for you and your mom. Just promise me you'll make it to the conference." Jenna was confused and skeptical. Why would Rebecca offer her money like it's not the most important thing someone has? "You don't even know me or my mom. So why would you offer this?" Rebecca smiled and said "That's true, but my heavenly father knows the both of you. I know he has a plan for you. Get some rest." Jenna watched as Rebecca left as if she was an angel. She began to reflect and consider the offer. Jenna felt so hopeful. She laid down and while the other girls were dancing and laughing, she fell asleep with the brochure in her hands and a smile on her face.

Chapter 4

Ishma

Be careful not to allow anyone to captivate you through an empty, deceitful philosophy that is according to human traditions and the elemental spirits of the world. - Colossians 2:8

Ishma is an honor student. Ishma is a D1 athlete. Ishma has a lot of good friends and is very popular. Ishma volunteers and drives unlike someone her friends in high school. Ishma is an atheist. Now, she wouldn't call herself that, she would explain it as not having a religion. Truth is, Ishma was so confused about what religion is and who God is. Growing up in a household that never practiced religious traditions she figured it was not real. She was actually taught that it was wrong. See to Ishma, religion was a tool, used to control people, make them spend money, live in fear, and trust a system controlled by the superiors in society. There was no spiritual reason for this theory on religion, it was political. It was easy to think this way. Also, she couldn't understand why anyone would believe in something they couldn't see. To her, there's just no way people are in clouds, or in a layer of earth never found. She was so confident in her beliefs. She was taught to be logical and to be against religious people because they would make her blind, deaf, and dumb to the world around her. She had many friends that had their own religion. At times she would challenge them to "help" them learn her truths. She had no concern on how offensive it could have been to people she called friends, people she should love and respect no matter their religious background.

During her lunch period one day, Ishma approached her friend Isaiah for wearing a necklace with a cross on it. "Why would you wear the murder weapon of someone you worship? That's a little condescending don't you think?" Isaiah was patient "Ishma, do you know what love is?" "What does that have to do with anything?" "Because this is not a murder weapon." Isaiah grabs his cross. "This symbolizes the most significant love of all. The love of God. Jesus knew he was going to be put on this cross. He knew he had to be the sacrificial lamb that God could use to wash away all of our sins… even those who don't love him back." Ishma did not expect so much conviction. It wasn't a big deal. Why did he take her question so seriously? She had so many questions, but Isaiah checked his phone and said "look, I have to go to class. Text my sister. You know she's working on the Christian conference next summer. She would probably enjoy answering your questions as much as you enjoy asking them." He headed off to class, and Ishma looked down at her phone because she received a text message.

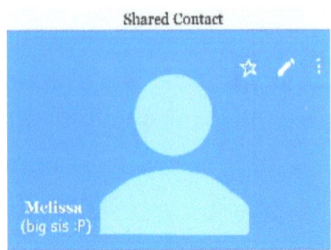

She looked up and he was gone. Later that day, Ishma was randomly thinking about what Isaiah was saying. She started to text his sister, Melissa. "Let's see if she can keep up" Ishma chuckled as she began typing:

> Hey Melissa! This is Ishma, Isaiah's friend. Do you remember me?

> What's up Ishma! I know you, I went to your game last night girl lol.

> Okay cool. Well I was talking to your brother about your God and religion. He had to run to class and told me to text you since you are doing some Christian thing next summer.

> Well, sure. I can answer your questions and tell you more about that event. You want to just come over today after school?

> Yeah sure I can do that, see ya later!

Once the final bell rang, Ishma gathered her things and started heading to Isaiah's and Melissa's parents' house. She got comfortable in the living room and kept small talk with Isaiah while she waited for Melissa to come downstairs. Melissa had a bible and notebook with some papers hanging out of it with her as she was grabbing some snacks and heading to Ishma. Before Ishma could even start talking, Melissa told her that they would equally respect each other's opinion. Laying that ground rule helped Ishma be more of a good listener instead of spitting out whatever came to mind.

These young ladies had a conversation for several hours. Ishma was so intrigued with how spiritual and yet political Melissa's viewpoint was. It was clear that Ishma was firm in her beliefs but was more understanding because of how Melissa communicated. Melissa made an offer that ultimately had a huge impact on Ishma. "I was wondering Ishma, I know you're not a Christian, but do you want to come with me to the God's Baby Girl conference? It could give you more information. Most girls from school will be there too! I saw the theater crew put out pretty lights and a dance floor girl!" Ishma thought about a conference as being a great place to network. She is very focused on receiving scholarship money for college and has always taken the opportunity to network. "Okay, I'll go. As long as nobody tries to convert me! It seems super fun and my friends will be there!"

She laughed and gave Melissa all her contact information to receive a ticket. Melissa chuckled with her and whispered to herself, "thank you God, I pray she makes this conference and more importantly, finds you." On her walk home, Ishma cut through a park that quickly became the neighborhood's sanctuary. She walked up to a park bench, laid on her back and began to count the stars. She requested answers from "the universe." "Now you, I can see, you're beautiful." She spoke to the stars about all her worries which was therapeutic to her, then she headed home.

Chapter 5

ADA

Love is patient and kind; Love does not envy or boast; it is not arrogant or rude. It does not insist on its own way; it is not irritable or resentful.
- 1 Corinthians 13 4-7

Tonight is going to be so awesome! The girls finally got together for a sleepover and it's long overdue. Ada, Elizabeth, Dakota, and Alexis are best friends and a little girl time is much needed to hang out with each other and catch up on the most talked about drama around, Ada and her new boyfriend. He's 6'2", a dancer, and very popular. All the girls in school wanted to be his girlfriend or at least get some attention from him. So, what makes Ada so special? "Okay sis, what's going on with you and Dylan? Are ya'll a thing or what?" Alexis went straight for the pink elephant in the room. "Well, you know..." Ada blushes and passes the popcorn. Dakota chimes in and says "no we don't know woman! Really, the coolest guy in school is all over you. I mean you're incredible and worth it so I can see what he sees in you but you're special enough for a real boyfriend. Don't you think he's too popular, maybe a playboy?" Ada laughed and said "I'm not even dating him. Nor am I that into him. It's pretty sweet that he cares so much about me that everyone notices." "YOU'RE A VIRGIN DUDE! Of course, he cares about you.

Have you ever taken a second to wonder what a 20-year-old is doing in the 10th grade with 15-year olds?" "Dakota chill." Beth interrupted. She typically keeps the peace between all the girls. But back to Dylan, yeah, a minor piece of information left out that changes this whole scenario. Ada saw past that detail, with his charming personality, his captivating dance moves, and how he made Ada feel protected from anyone. See, Ada has been though some sexual abuse and since she's 15 and he's 20, she saw that as a way nobody could hurt her again. Sure, it was a little strange and she didn't understand what he was doing as an adult and allowed to be a student in 10th grade. That was not her problem, maybe the school system but not hers. However, that didn't stop her from being with him. Besides, the attention was awesome. "Ada, seriously though, that guy is bad news," someone interrupted that thought. Ada paused the movie as if the girls were actually watching it to say "guys chill, he's cool, and if I need ya'll I promise I will come for all the advice I know ya'll have to give." The girls dropped it and Ada pressed play on the movie. Elizabeth, having to find a way to break the awkwardness, threw some of her gummy bears at Dakota's head. The girls laughed and hugged, then went back to having a much-needed sleep over.

The next day at school Alexis was walking down the hall and saw Ada and Dylan. They were kissing, out in the open which was very weird because Ada is classier than that, at least that's what Alexis thought. "Ewww! Get a room! See you at lunch girl!" Alexis laughed and walked to her next class, but Ada didn't find it funny. She knew she should not have been in public like that and her brother would be so mad, not to mention embarrassed. She quickly grabbed her stuff from Dylan's hand and headed to class. On her way to lunch Dylan came around the corner and told her he had a better idea for their lunch hour. He told Ada that it was so loud in the cafeteria and he wanted more alone time with her. She thought it was special and sweet but said "my friends are waiting for me. Dylan, you know we eat outside every day." With a confused look he responded, "okay but I thought we had a thing." I am doing all of this to make you feel important and special to me and it's like you don't want me to treat you right, like a man is supposed to.

Ada felt bad. She didn't know how a man was supposed to treat her since she was only 15 years old but at least he was trying. "Okay Dylan, I am sorry. We can do whatever you want, it is just one lunch period, and they will be okay. What Ada didn't know was that she was going to be taking these special lunch trips with Dylan everyday going forward. "Cool, come with me." Dylan took her to an empty classroom. Here they can be "themselves." Well, that's what Dylan told Ada. They spent these lunch hours getting to know each other. They shared so many scar stories and embarrassing parent stories that they could've started a television sitcom.

They really bonded and became best friends. So much so that Ada didn't really need to hang out with any other friend, so that meant she missed the last sleepover Dakota had at her house with all the girls. She only really began hanging out with them when she needed something it seemed. Elizabeth's parents were going to be gone this weekend and she was throwing the next sleepover. Ada asked if Dylan could come and that was the moment the girls knew she was no longer their friend; she was his girlfriend. Elizabeth was hurt and responded, "Well it's a sleepover, a girl sleepover. But sure if that'll get you to hang out with us." Perfect, Ada thought to herself, "I don't have to disappoint my girls and I don't get Dylan mad."

She was juggling a lot of pressure to be a good girlfriend, pressure to be a good friend, pressure to be a good sister, and of course, a good student. At the sleepover, she kicked back and just enjoyed the quality time. As the time went by it was soon to be bedtime. All the girls in one room and Dylan downstairs on the living room couch, keeping them safe. Ada was falling asleep and she got that much-predicted, almost too obvious text message, "you up?" that woke her right back up. The couple exchanged a few text messages and it wasn't long after that, Ada was exactly where Elizabeth didn't want her, downstairs with Dylan.

That night went as assumed and Ada lost her virginity to Dylan. That's the most personal she's let anyone to be to that point. This caused their relationship to not be like any other before, they were more connected. This meant that anything Dylan said went. Dakota would say it like this: "he's got her wrapped around his finger" the girls couldn't stand it. He was her identity. They were now upset about how distant she's been but because of what Alexis saw him do one day. "Ya'll today in social studies, Jeffery came in and was being his usual crazy tail, but guess what?" "You're going to tell us I'm sure."

The girls laughed at Dakota's smart response then Alexis said "Dylan hit her! Ada, in the head with his brush. It's like he got jealous because she was looking at Jeffery. Pissed me off!" The girls were surprised and upset like Alexis. "She was the toughest out of all of us, the most level-headed. Why would she just let him do that?"

Elizabeth said rhetorically. This time these girls weren't waiting until another possible, maybe sleepover, where Ada actually shows up. They stopped her in the hall, before she could get to Dylan. "Ada, something isn't right, please just talk to Mrs. Williams." She was more of a friend than a teacher. You could go to her about things you couldn't go to your parents about and all of the girls trusted her. "Ya'll might be right," Ada responded, surprisingly. It's like she knew this relationship was going downhill. "I will talk to her next period."

Ada had to swallow her pride to go into Mrs. Williams' class. But it was worth it because she needed the advice, she liked Dylan, but he was becoming more and more controlling and she couldn't stand the pressure to be perfect and the fear of not being that way. After telling Mrs. Williams, there was a silence. She was mostly in shock that out of any girl in school it was Ada who was this girl all the teachers knew as Dylan's girlfriend, who didn't mind PDA. She surely expected it to be one of the 18-year-old students and not her little precious Ada. "Oh sweetie, thank you for sharing this with me and trusting me with your personal life concerns. Dylan's a good kid but your right with your instincts. You shouldn't be dating him. Legally I should report this because of the age difference -" Ada interrupted "really Mrs. Williams? Please don't do that! It's not my fault he's allowed to be in my grade and he's in all of my classes."

Ada regretted talking to her and Mrs. Williams could tell. "But I won't. You need a friend right now and that's what I will be for you. Baby girl, you are a gift from God, and this is not what he said Love is. You shouldn't be afraid of someone that you love. You shouldn't have to justify why someone was cheating on you. You shouldn't have to sneak around the school with some boy because your family doesn't approve of him. A real man will respect you and not pull you away from your friends too." Mrs. Williams took that in when she said it and waited as she watched Ada, take it in too. "Look, why don't you just try to hang out with your girls for the rest of school. If he is still around and pursuing you by the summertime, give it another try. Fair?"

Mrs. Williams rubbed Ada's shoulder initiating a one arm hug. They agreed on that deal and Ada added that she will wait until after the conference coming up this summer called God's Baby girl. "I'm going with all of my friends so that will be the ultimate girl's trip too!" She said with life and that made Mrs. Williams smile. "Well I can't wait to hear about it." The bell rang; it was time to go to lunch.

Chapter 6

HANNAH

I wish that all were as I myself am. But each has his own gift from God, one of one kind and one of another. - 1 Corinthians 7:7

Hannah had a long day at school. Between normal classes, friends, and after school activities, she's pretty tired by the time she gets home typically. Today was the cherry on top for her. She rushed to her room once she got home and grabbed her diary. Writing set her at ease, she was able to pour out all the feelings she had, because sometimes talking about it is just too hard. Her mom told her about this new project she wants her to have ready soon. Let's just say she had a few words because of that.

Dear Diary,

Sometimes I wish I can just go to school during NORMAL hours and hang out with my neighborhood friends once school is out. All I do is work out early before school, travel to the different programs after school, and we even work on the weekends! Mom puts me in all these programs and it's a bit much sometimes. For starters, Mom put me in Junior ROTC. I still think it's because my older brother did it and it set him straight. What was Mom trying to do anyways? I'm not THAT bad... am I? LOL.

Secondly, Mom put me in the Junior Police Academy. I did just get promoted which is cool. Now that's wild!! It's crazy how I work with cops now. LOL, joke! But on a serious note, I really do love the amount of discipline they are teaching me. There are so many PT days, but it's okay because sometimes we do drills and have fun scenarios where we can arrest each other! My two favorite officers really believed in me though. By promoting me, that made me feel like I was expected to grow and keep climbing. They made me feel like I am full of potential and just need to be in the RIGHT POSITION to receive what life has to offer me.

Now I see what Mom is doing. I don't like doing all these extra-curricular activities, but I found the plus side. Mom is keeping me out of trouble. Not to mention, people really believe in me. Third one is kind of special. Mom puts me around people that are successful and serving. They make me feel like I can be successful and giving. Like Dr. Martha Bennet, a.k.a. OG Grinder, this woman knows how to get her money. She is always moving! And she knows EVERYONE too! The real cool thing is how much of a heart she has for people. I ain't never really thought good people could make a lot of money and can be rich. She helps EVERYONE, like how?? I really love people and it encourages me to stay true to that and serve more. Good people, one's that are caring and serving the community, can be successful, and receive wealth too.

But this lady is straight tripping. She is having me speak at an IBM conference... dude a WOMAN OF IBM conference! These are doctors, engineers, and scientist! I'm only 15 years old! It's going to be about 150 of them! Like lol that is super crazy! I did start writing already and I guess I am not that opposed to it. I mean... speaking in front of all those people would be cool! It's kind of scary but it does take me out of my comfort zone. See, Mom... she always forces or "recommends" these different programs. Lol, she's why people think so highly of me. Like that one coworker she has! I forgot her name, but she bought my ticket for God's Baby Girl this summer!!!! Crazy right?!? Yeah, she was telling my mom about how I am mature and respectful. All the good things, and then asked me what I had planned this summer.

I told her, "Well there is this conference that I am trying to raise money for. It's called "God's Baby Girl." She kept listening, so I kept talking, lol. "It's for ladies of all ages *wink wink*, to get together and identify the specific 'baby girl' God has destined her to be. The weekend will pretty much connect us all with similar life stories and goal-oriented games. And then a guest speaker..." She was so shocked! LOL and I'm not sure why. But then she said, "Well I guess your mom wouldn't mind if Molly and I join you two? And don't worry about the ticket, I will cover the rest for you!" Whaaaaaaaaaaa! LOL. What a blessing this lady is! I guess there are a lot of benefits from all these tedious programs. Sometimes I really do feel like I just want to be a student lol. But overall, I can *appreciate this. This crazy project with Dr. Bennet may not be that bad. I know I am strengthened and can get through it! Whelp, until tomorrow! I am getting sleepy and need to finish my speech!!!*

Love, Hannah

Just like that, Hannah starts working on that speech She spent hours on it and there was no time to even try to start on homework. She was so focused; she wrote until she fell asleep. Her mom walked past her room. She saw Hannah's head down on the desk and went in to wake her up. She notices the diary. After only two seconds, wondering if she should read her daughter's diary, she grabbed the book. What was a frown quickly turned into a smile and she began to look back at Hannah. It's a good feeling when a mom knows her daughter understands why she raised her that way. Her mom woke her up and sent her to bed. "You know you have to be up at 5:00 AM, I don't know why you are writing this late. Bedtime, now." Hannah grunted, and they both laughed right before saying good night to each other and going to bed.

Chapter 7

MARGARET

Because, if you confess with your mouth that Jesus is Lord and believe in your heart that God raised him from the dead, you will be saved. - Romans 10:9

SHE WAS FRUSTRATED. SHE WAS tired of not knowing. She just couldn't understand why she felt something she didn't believe. Margaret is a part of an entrepreneur group, which was a blessing she didn't see coming. They were people with principles and the one thing she noticed about them was they shared a belief she did not believe at that time. It wasn't everyone that believed the same literally, but it seemed as if all the people she was working with and became friends with were Christians. This was never a deal breaker for her because she was living in the south. Everyone she knew were Christians, or some variation of it she thought. She generalized any biblical references in her notes, and she noticed there was a lot to generalize. Margaret heard sayings like "all the honor and glory to my Lord and Savior Jesus Christ" from speakers on stage talking about their success. She thought it was such a "medieval times" thing to say and sort of chuckled every time she heard it.

The more she was studying to be more successful the more she noticed that it was not just the people in her group. A lot of the successful people she looked up to were also Christian. People like Steve

Harvey, Teri Savell Foy, and John Maxwell. Really, she noticed that most of the success principles she knew had biblical origins. Margaret would become curious and want to understand but was too stuck in her own ways that she'd usually just let it go. The entrepreneur group hosts leadership conferences 4 times a year and the conference that got her frustrated and tired of not knowing was the last one a couple of months ago. Something miraculous happened. These conferences are 3-day weekends, the first two days are mostly business, and the last one typically is a church service, then business.

Margaret never paid it any mind. Honestly, it gave her more time to sleep in and be refreshed for the business portion. This Sunday service was different. Margaret invited one of her friends and she wanted to go to the Sunday service. Margaret wanted her to experience the whole weekend and didn't want her to be lonely, so she went with her. She tried her hardest to not move to the music or hug a random stranger out of obligation because the pastor said so. Everything was fun and captivating, nothing too major. After all, Margaret knows when she's just having a good time. Towards the end of the service there was an altar call.

To Margaret's surprise, her friend went down. Okay here's her perspective. They are in a coliseum with thousands of people initially talking about making money and business and now they are spiritual and are singing "kumbaya", so it's already a bit overwhelming and awkward. Then the one person she was looking after runs down the bleachers into a mosh pit of crying people who just surrendered themselves to God. A God she did not believe in at that moment. Margaret knew what was expected of her. She had to follow her friend and comfort her. As Margaret ran after her friend, she was thinking to herself, "what am I doing? People are going to think I believe like them or worst they are going to judge me because I don't, and I am just going for a friend." She got to the pit and hugged her friend.

Suddenly, things became strange. Physically, she was lightheaded, and she felt like she was seeing fading clips of everything around her like in a movie. She started to look around and she felt alone, with a presence. She was in a room full of thousands of people, but she felt like she was alone with one other person that could see her, and she couldn't see them. Spiritually, she heard a voice that said, "I've come this far to get you here. I won't let go." There's no way. Did she just hear God? She couldn't understand because she did not literally hear a voice like someone was whispering in her ear but like it was inside her head. That's what makes it so hard for her to deny it. She doesn't know how to make sense of what happened, so she goes to her mentors.

Her mentor, the husband, is someone who happens to have gone to school for ministry. Also, not just any school, Liberty University, one of the top Christian universities in the country. She broke the silence in the car and said "so ya'll know I'm not a Christian, or whatever. But now I have some questions, what is it all about and why does everyone make such a big deal about it?" This opened the door for a long conversation they did not expect. See, when Margaret said that, they responded, "well no, we did not know you were not Christian. We just assume because of how you acted."

Nonetheless, they did not assume the responsibility to immediately convert her. They simply requested that she studied a movie called A Case for Christ. The movie did all the work from there, truly. What Margaret experienced was life changing. She transformed to a whole new person, never to go back to her old ways, like an overextended rubber band that lost its elasticity. There was a newfound love. She felt completed, like all her wonders in the world disappeared. Margaret can only think about learning more. She was on a new journey, one that would involve a lot of research. She was referred to a lady from a local church named Lisa.

One day, while Margaret was at work, she agreed to meet up with Lisa on her lunch break. They went to a local restaurant and had a long conversation. After asking all the questions Margaret had, Lisa had her own too. They came to an understanding and Lisa left her with a few thoughts. Why was she feeling so alone this whole time? If she died, what would happen to her soul? How can she really argue the facts, when they are more in the favor of who God is? Margaret finally took a leap of faith. She walked with Lisa to her car and got inside. This was a moment. Margaret did not know Lisa very long and she was already in her car getting ready to say a prayer.

Whelp! Here it is! "Um, Jesus, or God? I'm not really sure," she chuckled, "I never really prayed before, but I just wanted to say thank you for saving me. And I am sorry for denying you all these years. I surrender and give my life to you." It was short and sweet but enough, Lisa told her. Margaret left completely stunned with her decision, and one task, to tell someone what she prayed. She did not miss a beat. She got back to work from her lunch break and told her boss why she was late and what she did. From that point she wanted to know all that she could. Lisa invited her to a summer conference to share her story on stage! She was just so intrigued about Margaret's story she had to share her testimony at the conference "God's Baby Girl."

Part Two:
God's Baby Girl

Chapter 8

GOD'S BABY GIRL

... A time to weep, and a time to laugh; a time to mourn, and a time to dance. - Ecclesiastes 3:4

It's here, finally it's here. The conference everyone has been waiting on. God's Baby Girl weekend conference is finally here. All the attendees start to arrive. Angela was so fidgety, fixing her frizzy curly hair in the mirror while her mom was driving. Her mom interrupted her and said, "Angie, your hair is fine, now where is your ticket Principal Joyner gave you?" "It's right here Mom," she replied while still fixing her hair. "Okay, hold on to it, we are pulling in now." As they pulled in, Angela's eyes almost popped out of her head. "This place is enormous!" Angela yelled. She looked to her right and saw a huge "Welcome to God's Baby Girl" sign made from balloons and told her mom "this is exactly like the poster from school! Let's go!"

Angela rushed her mom to the ticket booth. While waiting in the line, Angela's friend from school, Brenda noticed her. Brenda tapped Angela's shoulder and said, "I like your shoes," "oh thank you" Angela smiled and complemented back on Brenda's hair. She replied "Thanks', my name is Brenda. What's yours? "Angel--" she began to respond but Brenda cut her off. "Uhm I have to go, but nice to meet you Angela." Brenda's mom grabbed her hand. It was her turn at the ticket booth.

"Hi there Queen, ticket please." That was one of the staff ladies. They referred to all girls as Queen and guys as Kings. Brenda handed her the tickets. "Queen, all parties have to be here before I can check you in. I see Mom, is Dad near?" The truth was, Brenda couldn't forgive her father, and neither could her mom. They left without him. That was good enough for the ticket lady, she let Brenda and her mom through. They were greeted with bubbles and sunglasses. The person that was giving that away was wearing a "God's Baby Girl" t-shirt, just like the ticket lady. Brenda's mom noticed a lady who looked very familiar and said, "Hi Janice." "Oh, hey Lisa! It's so good to see you out here, isn't it lovely?" "You're right, this is my daughter, Brenda," said Lisa. Janice is her coworker and they immediately made sure they had seats next to each other. "This is my daughter, Jenna." She nudged Jenna to say hi.

As Jenna was introducing herself, she saw a friend from school and got distracted. "Hi, my name is Jenna," she said as she was looking past Brenda towards her friend Ishma checking in. "Hey, I'm Brenda." Jenna smiled at Brenda and said to her mom" can I go talk to my friend over there? I'll come right back." Her mom said sure and dismissed her. Jenna went up to Ishma and said " Hey Ishma, girl what are you doing here?" "Oh, hey Jenna I'm just checking it out. Isaiah's sister Melissa invited me out."

Then Jenna asked, "Does she know that you're an atheist?" Ishma replied, "Of course she does, she said a lot of my questions will be answered here and plus she mentioned a lot of girls from school were coming, like you." "Well yeah, that's cool." Jenna shrugged to avoid talking about religion. "Ishma look!" Jenna shouted, "There's a photoshoot here!" The girls rushed over to the photo booth. "Hey Queens! How about some pictures? There's all kinds of accessories in that box for you to create the LOOK of the weekend!" How could the girls say no to a photo shoot? The girls put on as many sparkling, glittery, bright colored outfits together and started posing.

For a moment they forgot they were at a conference, they were just having so much fun at that time. Ishma noticed a group of girls with snow cones. She asked one of them where she got it. Ada responded, "there's a truck closer to the stage that's giving them away!" Ishma thanked Ada and took Brenda with her to get a snow cone. "You're welcome girl!" Ada said and waved goodbye. Ada and her friends got there early to help set up and basically help run the event. Well, that's how they felt at least. They picked up the trash, directed people to the right area, and reminded people when the show started.

"Remember Queens, the show starts at 6pm and it's the main stage in the back." Dakota said softly to a lady and her daughter sharing a hammock, avoiding the summer sun, and enjoying the view. These girls are a huge help. "Excuse me miss," Hannah's mom tapped on one of the girls. "Yes ma'am?" Alexis (another one of Ada's friends) asked the lady. "How do we find our seats? I am just a little lost." Alexis looked at her ticket to find the best route to go. Alexis directed them "okay, so seat B3- 4. That's right behind the dance floor. Go down this way, you'll see a tile dance floor. Go directly behind it and that's your column. Walk down until you are in row 3 and you are the 4th seat to the right. Enjoy ladies!"

Hannah thanked Alexis and escorted her mom, her mom's coworker, and Molly (the coworker's daughter) to their seats. As they were walking, Hannah noticed a lady shouting towards the girls that just helped them. "Ada!" Lisa shouted. She was the main coordinator of the event and was getting ready to put these girls to work. "Ada sweetie, this is Margaret. She will be speaking tonight and sharing her testimony. Please host her and make sure she is sitting with you ladies. I need her backstage at 6:45 pm." Ada welcomed Margret and exchanged a hug with Lisa, as if that was payment for the favor. Margaret was in for a surprise. The girls took her to the dance floor and got her way out of her comfort zone. Line dancing was her favorite and Margaret had a great time. She made some cool friends and almost forgot about her testimony she had to share and how nervous she was. Once she got to her seat, she felt confident in her new decision to dedicate her life to Christ. She is so excited for the weekend and this journey to come. After the girls grabbed a few refreshments, they sat at their seats and got ready for the show. The stage lights came on and Margaret clenched her speech. The show was about to begin.

Chapter 9

Forgiveness

Be kind to one another, tenderhearted, forgiving one another, as God in Christ forgave you. - Ephesians 4:32

Be kind to one another, tenderhearted, forgiving one another, as God in Christ forgave you. Ephesians 4:32 The last video was ending on the screen and it was time for the next speaker. Angela and Brenda were sitting next to each other and were talking. The speaker immediately caught their attention with her opening statement. "If you are angry with someone who did something to hurt you- even if they don't know they hurt you- then listen up." Angela thought about all the people who took one look at her and judged her by her hair texture, skin, or even lifestyle. She thought of the girls that were supposed to be her friends but just used her and made fun of her. Brenda thought about her dad and the sexual abuse he put her through and listened up.

The speaker continued "In Ephesians 4:32 we are told to be kind to each other, TENDERHEARTED, forgiving each other like God in Christ forgave us. Let's do an exercise, say this with me: God forgives me, and I forgive me. I can forgive anyone who trespasses against me." Angela couldn't fathom forgiving the people that bullied her. It hurt too much. She had built up pain and anger. Just like Brenda. How could her father, the man who was supposed to protect her get away with molesting her, multiple times for multiple years? The speaker continued with that point, "I know it's hard. How could you be kind to someone who was cruel to you? How can you have a tender heart if people keep pushing you to be resentful, hesitant, and judgmental? When you are victimized you are left with the results of the abuse, not the abuser. They did what they wanted to, regardless of your feelings. That hurts on top of the abuse that you went through. You are left with the pain, shame, disgust, fear, and even guilt at times. So how do you turn those feelings into kindness and tenderheartedness? Well, you don't, in fact you can't. They don't coexist.

Do this: picture two roads. When something happens and someone hurts you, it is like they drove you straight to the beginning of where the two roads broke apart. One side is the pain, shame, disgust, fear and even guilt. You're in control of this route. You just have to keep those feelings as long as you stay on the road. On the other side- you know where I am headed don't you- the other road is where you choose Christ. You can give God your trust. That other road is full of peace, love, pride, and joy. Kindness and tenderness comes as a byproduct of these new reviving feelings. Even though we are told to forgive, and we will be forgiven, to forgive each other like Christ forgave us, we still have a choice, we still have free will."

Angela really wanted to feel the peace and pride the speaker was talking about. She was constantly anxious about her appearance. She would always feel like people are looking at her. She was not confident in her own skin. Same for Brenda, she just wanted to have a relationship with her father like before. She would be jealous of girls that had a good relationship with their dads, she just wanted a normal life. Brenda would constantly feel like people were watching her too but not for the same reason as Angela. She saw her body as a tool to get what she wanted. The girls looked at each other and noticed that they are both trying to process having to forgive people. They both smiled in support of one another and paid attention to the speaker. "The time is now. Release the pain and forgive the person." That mumbled in the background of

Brenda's mind like a song stuck in your head and you can't get it out, "release the pain and forgive the person."

The speaker encouraged the audience to use the blank sheet of paper that was given to them at the beginning of the talk. She had them write down who hurt them, why it hurts, and that they will forgive them for their own healing. The girls began writing. Bianca and Tiffany's name was written down among other girls and teachers at Angela's school. Being bullied and prejudged hurts. She just wanted people to get to know her for who she is and not for what she looks like. Angela found out that God makes no mistakes and she was made intentionally. Her frizzy curls, bronze skin and light brown eyes are just part of the custom wrapping of the gift to the world she is. She now can see clear as day, other people's opinion of her does not define who she actually is. She can finally forgive everyone she needs to since it does not hurt her anymore, she is healed.

As for Brenda, there was only one name she needed to write down. Her father's name. She thought she could trust him out of all people and that he would protect her. She was stuck in thought because how could he use her, lie to her, violate her, terrify her, and sexualize her, all while being her dad. The cool dad, the one everyone thought Brenda was lucky to have. Brenda reminded herself that she was going to come to this conference and grow. She wrote it down. "I forgive you dad for sexually abusing me and betraying our relationship." She was healed. She learned her worth and what God thought of her. The speaker continued, "that took strength and courage. I want to take a second to address that. Thank you for participating. Now, crumble that paper up and throw it on the ground. Go on!" The crowd began to look at each other and laugh at the ridiculous order, it seemed so silly. Everyone began crumbling their forgiveness letters, making a loud rumbling noise. It sounded like 1000 cicadas were having a party, then a shower of crumbled papers hit the ground.

"Great, you've acknowledged the wrong someone has done to you.

You've written in your own words that you forgive them. You've crumbled and threw that page on the ground, sealing the deal. It is done, my friends. You have done all you need to heal from that pain. God will handle the rest. He wants you to live with peace. With joy, knowing that he is in control. Know that there is an enemy that uses people to go against God's children. This enemy wants to kill, steal, and destroy. What he cannot destroy, he will distract. Do not let this pain and this offense that the person did distract you from living in your full purpose. Thank you." What a note to leave on! The girls looked at each other, both having tears rolling down their eyes. They were healed. The lights lowered and another fun video played it's time for the next speaker.

Chapter 10

ABSTINENCE

"For this is the will of God, your sanctification: that you abstain from sexual immorality; that each one of you know how to control his own body in holiness and honor, not in the passion of lust like the Gentiles who do not know God...." - 1 Thessalonians 4:3 ESV

As the last video began to close, a song came up to introduce the next speaker. It made most of the audience laugh because of how awkward and inappropriate it seemed. A lot of the people there came with their parents and now Salt-N-Papa, "Let's Talk about Sex" is playing and it's hard to ignore. Ada and Jenna ended up standing in the back laughing themselves into stomach aches. Ada was throwing her snow cone trash away and Jenna was walking back from the bathroom. They both decided to stand in the back to stretch their legs out, anything to not go back to their parents during that song.

The opening song was coming to an end and the speaker began, "Ahhh how awkward was that guys? I mean come on!" The speaker is energetic and laughing hysterically, setting everyone at ease instantly. "Okay okay calm down crazy people! I am so excited to be sharing with you all today." Ada and Jenna headed back to their seats at that point.

They realized they were on the same row and laughed at the odds. "I want to talk to you all today about living a fulfilled life and having healthy relationships that's pleasing to God. I know I opened up with this silly song, and you probably thought we were going to talk about sex only. There are a couple of relationships that you must consider before we even get to sex. Which we will talk about. For starters, how is your relationship with God? Whether you know him like the back of your hand or haven't seen evidence of his existence yet. How is that relationship? How about your relationship with yourself? Do you know yourself and love yourself or has it been a long time since the real you showed themselves? Finally, how is your relationship with society? That is everyone outside of your circle. Your circle being you and God of course. Are you finding your identity and even the identity of God from your inner circle or from society? You know, the world around you has a lot to say about the world in you. Who you are is only identified by what God says about you and how you interpret that. However, it is very hard to see it like that. I know. We often care too much about what other people think about us and not about who we actually are."

The speaker paused; this was a moment of seriousness. "Look, I am not here to give you positive affirmation over and over again. Make you feel amazing and next weekend it's back to reality. I want to just share my story, that's what I know best. Also, I do want you to know that you are valuable, and God purposefully made you exactly how you are. I had to learn who I am too, and I am still learning so don't be too hard on yourself." Jenna pulled her hair back behind the ears and smiled slightly, almost relieved at the thought of not having to carry the burden of embarrassment and shame. For the first time she started thinking, "what if God does see me? What if it didn't matter that I was homeless and that everywhere I went the group home team went with me?"

The speaker grabbed her attention again, "Okay, okay, let's get into it! Your relationship with God. The reason why we have to start there is because you might not understand the importance of abstaining from sex until marriage, if you don't understand the why behind that seemingly impossible to follow rule!" The crowd laughed again as she made the sex talk super light and less about sex. She continued, "In the beginning of time, God made man and saw that was not good enough for complete fulfillment. So, he made woman.

These are cliff notes by the way because you are responsible for your own knowledge so you can fill in the blanks to that story by doing research in the book of Genesis." It seemed like the parents really like that idea of allowing their children to teach themselves and not always learn only when someone is telling them to. "You are his creation. I know in a room like this some of y'all don't understand or even believe. But the most beautiful thing about our creator is that he still loves us regardless of that fact. It is the ultimate unconditional love and that is important. Our relationship with the creator, God that made us to his likeness, is sacred and purposeful. In the Holy Bible, God explains how we can have a healthy relationship with him. How would you like to show your appreciation to our creator? Would you want to stay in good standing with the one who pieced you together cell by cell and strand by strand perfectly in his eyes? I do too!

That's why I am standing here telling my story. I am constantly surprising myself in the middle of a bible study because God is telling me to do one thing and I vividly remember all the times I've done the exact opposite. The biggest 'aha' moment I had like that was a few years back. I began reading about sexual purity and realized I was not living up to par. I was living with a longtime boyfriend and we were not waiting for marriage if you know what I mean." Ada bashfully smiled as she was thinking about Dylan. Jenna was not too far behind. Their simultaneous reactions set off another laugh, these girls knew what she meant.

The speaker chuckled at the innocence of the girls and continued. "I told him one day ' now that I am saved, I want to do this right. I want to abstain from sex until we get married.' He respectfully declined. I realized that he was okay with dating me when I was atheist, so how could I be upset with him for not wanting to do this together?" Ada was serious for a moment and realized that Dylan probably wouldn't go for that either. With the age difference Ada always felt like she had to keep up with other girls, so she knows if she takes that away from him, he may not like her as much. But wait…. Ada stopped and thought about what the speaker was just saying.

Dylan was not on a path of growing his life to align with God's word. So, what was more important? God or Dylan? The speaker continued, "I quickly learned that this is not the guy that will help me grow my relationship with God, help me find my purpose, and be my rock when I am weak and fall short to the sins of this world. And besides, what about me? I had to think about my relationship with myself. I knew I was right, but I felt so bad. He would tell me things like 'God forgives' and 'we all are sinners, all you have to do is repent.' I knew I wanted everything God had to offer me and after being saved I was not going to let anyone stop that. So, I had to leave my longtime boyfriend and start fresh. I took time for my singleness. There was a need for me to learn to love myself and learn to realize that I am enough all by myself. During that time, I found hobbies I never knew I liked, I gained so many cool friends, and I was really about my money, okay!" Jenna was excited because she knew there were so many things she wanted to try but wouldn't because she wanted to stay cool. Now that Jenna is able to take time for her singleness, she can now date herself and learn who she is, she decided to take full advantage of that. The speaker continued, "Finally, my relationship with society. I was torn between the fantasy of being in an attractive relationship for all my peers and establishing a respect for myself and my values for my elders.

There were so many different 'right ways to live' and I always felt as if I was getting it wrong. Abstinence became important to me because I realized other people's voices blocked out God's. We as people can justify as much as we want for the reasons we do things. Once you know that it's simply right from wrong, you have a choice." Ada, taking a deep breath, realized that she has just been going through society motions. She didn't want to live her life just for other people but to reap the benefits of living for God, she decided to leave Dylan for good. Jenna decided to block out the noise from society, to listen to God and allow herself to live free.

The speaker closed by saying, "I want you all to take some time to think about those three relationships. God, yourself, and society. I want you to have the freedom I have when I put these relationships in that order of priority. Lastly, I want to leave you with this. You do not have to aspire to be married just yet, but like I said, it's my story. After I took time for my singleness, I met someone." By this time, the audience was well engaged and let out a huge "AWWWWW," the speaker laughed. "Yes, yes. I met a man who kept himself in God's presence. I was attracted by so many things but the one thing that locked me in so early in our relationship is that he was willing to move closer to God with me. I told him that I was abstaining from sex and waiting until marriage. He understood my reasons and saw it as a way to grow spiritually for himself as well. He's a man that respects me, honors God, and makes selfless decisions for our best interests. When I stopped focusing on other people and I centered my attention on God and his plan for my life that's when the true blessings came. It is worth the wait and it is worth the discipline. We started dating obviously and one day we crossed the line... that's right, we did it." The crowd laughed and listened in for more "and you know what else? When I cried because of how bad I felt he didn't say things like 'God forgives' and 'we all are sinners, all you have to do is repent,' he prayed over us. Yep right there, right after everything. He prayed and promised to try and keep out all temptation. He later went on to rededicate his life to Christ in a commitment to living obediently. That does not have to be the man you want. My point is, he is the man God made for me. The man that God made for you is out there. You just have to follow his plan to meet him.... It's been great talking to you guys! Ya'll were wonderful. Also, for all the people who are not going to follow my advice, please use protection at all times!" The crowd stood up and clapped as the speaker left the stage. Margaret quickly went to the bathroom to calm her nerves. She was up next. She was about to share to the world how she started her journey in this new found faith. The lights go dim and a video begins introducing Margaret.

Chapter 11

SALVATION

"If you confess with your mouth that Jesus is Lord and believe in your heart that God raised him from the dead, you will be saved. For with the heart one believes and is justified, and with the mouth one confesses and is saved." - Romans 10 9-10

THE LIGHTS SLOWLY BEGAN TO brighten the room more and more as Margaret walked on stage to begin. She was nervous, mostly because she cared about what people thought of her. At this point it was going to happen and she suddenly realized that she couldn't turn back now. She was standing in front of a large crowd, so large there were people still doing activities behind the crowd and it did not interrupt the speakers at all, they couldn't even tell. It was silent, so she began " uhm... hello. My name is Margaret and I'm 22 years old. I suppose you can say I've always been a spiritual person but just not religious. I still consider it that way, but I'll get into that. I was raised with a literal and scientifically themed practice. It was what catapulted my curiosity in life. My family was by default named atheist. Atheism is the disbelief in God's existence. I only saw God as a fictional creature that, when the story is told right, can control mass groups of people. This was taught to me at an early age, so I just carried that thought process throughout my life and was not affiliated with any religions. However, I was spiritual. I always had this child-like faith that I would know how I came to existence."

Ishma was relating so well to Margaret. Everyone knows her as the atheist at school and that she has no eternal future as people told her. Ishma felt at ease because now someone else understood where she was coming from. She felt like the only person in the world to doubt God and now she knows she isn't. This empowered her to listen more to Margaret's story. Margaret continued, "I remember parking my car in a parking lot surrounded by tall grass, and just talking to the sky. The universe. I knew there was something out here bigger than us. I think most of us can agree on that. The 'what' is what gets tricky? I just didn't want to believe in what society wanted me to believe in because I was told to. I felt confident in my belief and I felt certain that everyone believed what they believed because of where they are from. It seemed that religion was culturally based, and my logic was this: if the truth depends on geographical location and generational rituals, then it's not really truth, it's just perception."

Ishma's eyes were stuck on Margaret. It's like they were the only ones at the event. There was truth in what she said. The Europeans portray the world's Savior Jesus Christ to look like them, which he did not, and the majority of the people in this world is reading God's word in their own language with transcribed interpretation when the original language of God's word is Hebrew, which is nowhere near English. So, over the years of fitting the truth into culture for common understanding makes the category of religion a melting pot of truth and perception from all over the world. Margaret continued, "What I was not expecting was an undeniable spiritual experience to happen to myself. I wasn't looking for anything specific, especially not a God to look up to. Being an atheist is simply living without incorporating theology in your life, in my opinion. I'd like to explain it like this, raise your hand if you ever experienced something and told someone about it, with the hope that they will take your word and go experience it themselves."

She paused and the audience all slowly admitted to peer pressuring someone. Margaret nodded her head and smiled then said, "Awesome, same here. Now think about the other person's perspective of your incredible experience. There is no clue why it was so necessary for them to experience, no clue about how you feel towards it, genuinely because they never experienced it; just no connection when you first introduce it to them. That was me, I was that person. I was not introduced to any religion let alone God because my family saw it as a tool for oppression."

Ishma thought that there was no way a girl actually thought like her for starters, and now that girl went to the other side. Ishma was enjoying the event because of its aesthetics and girly vibe, but now she is engaged and frustrated because she agrees with Margaret. Ishma is wondering where Margaret is headed. Margaret continues "I was taught, and I believed that there was no God, period. That's how I lived, not searching, not feeling lost, just living. I justified my beliefs by saying all religions 'coexisted' and I was for all people, so all beliefs are right.

However, the problem with that is that there is a sacrificial savior named Jesus Christ and he is King. Nobody can deny him and the spirit of God touching all our people. God is the same God in all of your battles and all of your victories. I quickly began to realize that. I was never alone. I have free will and that's why God let me stumble across him the way I did. It was not my planned choice and that's exactly what makes his power so undeniable.

Finally, the clarity and the peace." Margaret paused, Ishma was crying uncontrollably it seemed. She couldn't figure out why she just kept crying. It was almost embarrassing, but then Ishma looked around and saw almost all the other girls her age crying too. She made eye contact with Margaret and Margaret smiled. She knew that feeling Ishma was going through, she felt it herself. As she continued speaking Hannah grabbed Ishma by the hand. No, they did not know each other. That didn't matter, there was an instant connection. A sisterhood. Margaret continued, "I came here today because I wanted to understand more about God and how he works through other people like me. I thought sharing my story would be a nice 'in between the main speakers' speech but no. I now realize that God is using me to reach someone hearing my voice. There's so much joy here, and love that I feel. Embrace this moment because it could change the rest of your lives. I pray that whatever challenge you are facing that's going against God has no more strength to fight. That your subconscious mind no longer is just this awesome human phenomenon, but it becomes a relationship between you and the spirit of God that lives in you once you accept him."

Ishma clenches her jaws and fist as tight as possible, and then releases. She fell into Hannah's arms and continued to weep. Ishma gave up. There was no outburst, no direction to pray from the speaker, just her surrendering. Margaret was leaving off the stage and all Ishma could remember her saying as she was closing was "don't let this weekend just be an undeniable spiritual experience. Go seek the voice that has guided you to this very moment." As the lights were dimming, Ishma quickly went to the restroom to wash her face.

Chapter 12

WHO IS GOD'S BABY GIRL?

"You are a Child of God... You are wonderfully made, dearly loved and precious in his sight. Before God made you, he knew you... there is no one else like you!" – Psalm 139

THE LIGHTS BEGAN TO COME on and a disco themed light show began with fun music. Ishma walked back to her seat and tried to thank Hannah for being there for her when she was crying. It was too hard for Hannah to hear Ishma thank her, so she smiled, shrugged her shoulders, and said "girl, don't worry about it! Just dance." Then she grabbed Ishma hand and started moving it with no rhythm all over the place to encourage her to dance! Ishma caved and got out of her emotional mood, the two were dancing until the next speaker came up to the stage. A host came up to introduce the next speaker.

"Now we get to hear from the author, Tiane Sutton. She will explain what it means to be God's Baby Girl, introduce you to a movement, and encourage you all to live in your truth. "She came to the stage and began the closing speech for God's Baby Girl conference." Hi everybody! My name is Tiane and I am so excited to share with you all today! I just want to thank everyone for being a part of my vision. This has been an amazing journey for me, and I am honored to have a few more moments of your time! I am grateful for the chance to be authentic and share pieces of my life with everyone free of judgement. I really encourage you to open up about hard topics in your life. It is very liberating.

So, let's get started! I will have you all out and heading to our dance party in no time!" The crowd looked up with a surprised look like a kid at an amusement park. Tiane continued "yeah I said it... surprise! Only for people who feel like staying and having some summer fun of course, no pressure! I just want to cover a few things. For starters, 'God's Baby Girl' is a phrase I came up with as I was writing the book. Just about in the middle of the process. Ultimately, it's the ladies that confessed Jesus Christ as her Lord and savior, providing access to God's presence and eternal kingdom. We are his creation and once we accept the Lord, we can acknowledge our father/daughter relationship with God. There are no specifics to appearance, lifestyle, or ethnicity. The list goes on honestly. There are no Earthly stereotypes as God's baby girl. Please free your mind from all the noise in the world. It is simple. It is internal sis; you are God's baby girl. Now, let's rejoice! This scripture helps me put the community of people you are a part of in context from God's word: 'So then you are no longer strangers and aliens, but you are fellow citizens with the saints and members of the household of God, built on the foundation of the apostles and prophets, Christ Jesus himself being the cornerstone, in whom the whole structure, being joined together, grows into a holy temple in the Lord. In him you also are being built together into a dwelling place for God by the Spirit' - Ephesians 2:19-22. So, what does that mean?"

The speaker pauses to give everyone a chance to read the lengthy scripture on the screen. Let's revisit that verse: So then you are no longer strangers and aliens, but you are fellow citizens with the saints and members of the household of God, built on the foundation of the apostles and prophets, Christ Jesus himself being the cornerstone, in whom the whole structure, being joined together, grows into a holy temple in the Lord. In him you also are being built together into a dwelling place for God by the Spirit.

Tiane began speaking again. "We are no longer strangers. We are a community, women of all ages, who can share the gospel and live our God-given dreams. I really want you to grasp that. Do not leave this conference today without meeting someone you did not know before coming here. You can lean on God's Baby Girl, the community, for anything. Chances are we have been through what you are going through or know someone that has answers for you. I am saying this because a lot of women feel like they are going through life alone. Yes, as you can see from my testimony, there are things that should never happen to anyone and it takes years of healing from. However, your sisters are your safe place.

Ladies, let's have an open conversation about real issues, let's walk with our sisters, hand in hand, through any obstacle she needs support with. We are called to come together and glorify his holy name. Is it safe to say that regardless of what personal issues you are currently going through, you still have a future to work towards? The future is not promised true, but your future is expected to come. From grade school to grad school and beyond, we all have goals for our lives. So, don't look at this community as only a safe place for hard times, but also a resource center for your growth. Lean on each other.

Lastly, how can we give back?" She stopped and put a slide on the screen with a picture of the Earth. This helped the audience realize how many other people were in great need. She continued, "This is our home, but we treat it like an Airbnb. I encourage everyone to drop a global issue we can tackle in the 'change the world' box here on stage. Whoever wants to serve our community with us I thank you. In the effort of keeping peace and looking out for all of God's children, we can actively make a difference.

God gave each one of you a special gift. Strengthen it. Don't let anyone ever take your dreams, goals, and aspirations away from you. We can give back by using our God given talent, our strength in this sisterhood, and the power of the Holy Spirit. I encourage everyone to work on a project you've always wanted to explore but was worried what people thought of you. Let this conference be the reset point in life. I hope you took what you needed from this conference and this is just the beginning of your journey. Thank you!"

Tiane left the stage and the host began closing "Wow, what a powerful conference. Please don't forget to grab your belongings right away. As you leave this section, your seats are going to have a dance party for those of you that want to hang around some more! Grab anyone with a 'God's Baby Girl' t-shirt on if you have any questions. Have a great day everyone!"

The End.

NOTES

NOTES

NOTES

NOTES

NOTES

Forgiveness

NOTES

Who hurt me?

_____

Why it hurts?

I will forgive you because…

Letter to God...

Write about the day you decided to give your life to Christ and trust God.

Share your story…

About the Author

Tiane Sutton grew up in the South Bronx, New York, then moved to Raleigh, North Carolina, with her family in her teens. Once atheist, Tiane dedicated her life to Christ in May 2018. She recently got married in January 2020. Recently added to the board of directors for Cover my Sisters, Tiane works closely with the author of "No Makeup" Charletta Denise. Tiane is a first-time author. God's Baby Girl is her first published book and has plans on expanding from there. Ultimately, Tiane has plans to start a ministry that will provide aid and consult to people who have childhood traumas to overcome.

Contact Information:

Email: Tianesutton@godsbabygirl.co
Instagram: @tianesutton
Facebook: Tiane Sutton

His Glory Creations Publishing, LLC is an International Christian Book Publishing Company, which helps launch the creative works of new, aspiring and seasoned authors across the globe, through stories that are inspirational, empowering, life-changing or educational in nature, including poetry, journals, fiction and non-fiction.

DESIRE TO KNOW MORE?

Contact Information:

CEO/Founder: Felicia C. Lucas

www.hisglorycreationspublishing.com

Email: hgcpublishingllc@gmail.com

Phone: 919-679-1706

www.ingramcontent.com/pod-product-compliance
Lightning Source LLC
Chambersburg PA
CBHW042331150426
43194CB00001B/16